In Repair

From Existing to Living

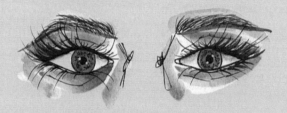

A Story in Poems
by

SARAH LYNN

IN REPAIR

FROM EXISTING TO LIVING

Sarah Lynn

Poet | Recovery Advocate | Author

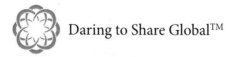 Daring to Share Global™

Published by Sarah Lynn,
February 2021 - 9781777571801

Editor: Diana Reyers
Typeset: Greg Salisbury
Book Cover Art: Isabelle Vaux
Artwork: Jade Dekker & Isabelle Vaux

DISCLAIMER: Readers of this publication agree that, neither Sarah Lynn nor, Diana Reyers will be held responsible or liable for damages that may be alleged as resulting directly or indirectly from the use of this publication. Neither the lead publisher nor the self-publishing author can be held accountable for the information provided by, or actions, resulting from, accessing these resources.

DEDICATION

You are brave, loving, and resilient.
This book is for you mom.

TESTIMONIALS

I have known Sarah Lynn her entire life; I have watched her journey from the happy carefree child she started as to the confused, depressed, anxious and troubled teen.
I've watched Sarah go from the "light" to the "dark" and then work her way back to the "light".
Her repair journey was tougher than you'd ever want to see anyone go through,
least of all someone you love dearly.
As you read Sarah's amazing baring of her soul you will see her transition back from the "dark." Her intention, apart from her own recovery, of sharing her thoughts and emotions is to help others that are struggling.
While sometimes the words are dark they are meant to share how bad and destructive one's mind can be with the ultimate intention to show that everyone's feelings are real to them and in these sort of illness, normal.
Most importantly though it is meant to show that there is light at the end of the tunnel if you are prepared to work hard and to tell the reader that there is help out there for those that are suffering.
The dark times are familiar, in which there is comfort, and the light is new and scary, but as Sarah writes it is worth the battle, just reach out and ask for help, it's out there waiting for you.
If Sarah's sharing and baring of her soul will help even one other

person, then part of her mission will be accomplished.
Sarah hopes to continue her journey while helping others be
successful on theirs, and I have every confidence
she will succeed at that as well.
Thankfully Sarah is brave and courageous,
she has learned to re-design
her emotions and her visions and to love who she is.
I shall forever be so very proud of Sarah and admire the
determination and success she has achieved on her journey.

~ Anne Carswell Taylor

Overcoming mental illness, trauma, or heartbreak
isn't a straight path.
It has turns and detours, oftentimes taking you
right back to where you started.
That is exactly what Sarah achieves in "In Repair."
True, unbridled emotion pours off of every page.
She doesn't flinch away from the dark and ugly bits
that accompany suffering .
In Repair shows readers that, for many of us, finding our way
back to ourselves and our happiness (as ever-fleeting as it may be)
is an ongoing battle.
Sarah's poems lay bare the truth that some days
our demons consume us and
other days the light shines through clearer than before.
But in the end, no matter how hard it was and will continue to be,
that battle is worth it.

~ Rachel Wehniainen

Sarah Lynn has put her heart, mind, and soul into this
devastatingly original anthology.
Her words will take you on an emotional roller coaster
as she reveals her own
transformation from troubled teen to vulnerable, sage adult.

~ Lisa Martin,
Best-selling author of Briefcase Moms

IN THANKS

The support I received from the people around me is
astounding. To everyone who was there for me in any way,
big or small, I thank you. There are two people I would like
to give my gratitude to specifically, Isabelle Vaux and Melissa
Ander. No matter how hard I try, I am unable to write poetry
about them because I have no words to express
my feelings for them.

Izzy,

You are my soul mate. You make me happy I am alive. You
stayed when I was so fucked up I couldn't function. You are
normal, and you loved me when I was far from it. You don't
recognize how beautiful of a human you are, inside and out.
You are gorgeous, intelligent, loving, hilarious, beautiful, and
the perfect human in every way possible. Believe in yourself.
You recognize your intelligence, so try to see your beauty;
you have both in spades.
I love you more than anything or anyone.

Melissa,

You saved my life. You never gave up on me when I tested
every single boundary you had. I tried to make you leave me
to prove to myself I wasn't lovable – but you didn't. You were
the first person who stood up to my bullshit, and
you refused to be scared of me.
My resilience bloomed when I met you.
I love you so much.
Always

PROLOGUE

I was a sensitive child, thinking that almost everything was sentient. Before life happened, I was full of energy; I was playful, creative, and always full of joy. Waking up every day came easy. A fire fuelled by excitement burned so brightly inside me. Everything I owned was pink, and my personality consisted of squealing laughter and loving the world. I viewed everything as shiny and sparkly.

As I got older, my feelings became mixed up in my mind, leaving me uneasy about my interactions with the universe. I wanted so badly for my body to feel calm and at ease. I elevated my emotions to, what felt like, another level. What I didn't realize was that not everyone experienced feelings the same way I did.

I am the firstborn of triplets: two girls and a boy. We have our separate friends and individual dreams like everyone else does. When I was little, I was aware there was a sort of expectation we would all be the same, and I assumed we all had equal abilities and feelings. Elise and James were not as sensitive as I was, and I took their teasing to heart. By the time my peer group hit 11 and 12 years old, all they wanted was to be grown up. All I wanted was to feel loved and accepted. Kids do not always understand how being cruel affects another the way adults do. I wanted to stay safe in my bubble of being a child and not face the world.

I had a very tough time dealing with conflict. Our house was always busy, noisy, and filled with schedules. Having a parent with a short temper did not match well with me. Disapproval of any sort, or anything I perceived as disapproval, made me feel less and less worthy of living or having an opinion. I felt like I had to be perfect, *Happy, Smiley, Polite,* and that any fault I experienced made me a disappointment. I dealt with trying to calm my nervous system by avoiding anything that could cause conflict, staying silent, and doing everything to avoid being a nuisance.

When I experienced anxiety at the age of 11, I began therapy. It was taking over my life; my schoolwork, my friendships, my family. My confidence took a major hit. I genuinely believed no one wanted me. Over the years, a multitude of disorders came rearing to a head, being diagnosed with and managing everything from Borderline Personality Disorder, Obsessive Compulsive Disorder, Anxiety, Complex-Post Traumatic Stress Disorder, Depression, Attention Deficit Hyperactivity Disorder, Anorexia to a dissociative disorder.

By the time I was almost 17, the therapist I saw for five years told me she was no longer equipped to help. I was suicidal, depressed, and self-harming. The fear of abandonment was one of my core issues; it felt like a confirmation of my belief that I was unlovable. In my mind, this reiterated I wasn't and would never be good enough for anyone. I hated everything about being alive, and I didn't want to see anyone or anything. Feeling completely broken and useless, I saw eight different therapists over the next few months; I did not resonate with any of them. Even at that age, I was able to read people. Connection was a huge thing for me, and I have come to learn that for me, that is about feeling truly seen.

I met Melissa, my long lasting therapist, about two months after I turned 17. My uncle just died, the most important friendship to me at the time was on the rocks, I wasn't talking to my dad because of an incident that had happened between us, and I just tried to kill myself for the first time. She was honest, and she wasn't scared of me. In the past, I used others' fear of me to my advantage in order to keep my *secrets*. We spent the next seven months together in her office twice a week. Throughout that time, I was figuring out my sexuality, drinking, developing an eating disorder, and I refused to take her advice while continuing to self-harm. I wasn't telling her shit, and I wasn't ready to change. All I needed was someone to listen and believe in me. Then one day, I showed up at her office after downing a bottle of pills and alcohol. She gave me hell, and then gave me to the hospital, but she didn't give up on me.

In a weird kind of way, Melissa broke me by refusing to give up on me. She broke me into a breakthrough. It was after that when I started being honest with her. I convinced her and my family I was stable enough to go to university, and it seemed like a good idea in my head. As it turns out, that was the only place it was a good idea. In September 2017, I moved to Quebec. Within a week, my mental health started to decline. My self-harm went from moderate to extreme, and I slept all day and stayed up all night -then I discovered purging. I lasted maybe a month and a half before trying to kill myself again.

After ending up in a Quebec psych ward where no one spoke English, I came home from university. I felt like a total failure, not knowing what I wanted to do or who I was. Looking back, I don't think I ever really knew who I was. I certainly had my own personality, but I had moulded it to what I thought everyone around me wanted it to be. To keep myself occupied, I worked at my mom's office part-time and saw Melissa again in person. At this point, I decided to try getting my life together; self-harm was a big thing stopping me, so I decided to get clean and stop cutting myself.

For years I struggled with body dysmorphia and disordered eating, and unfortunately, as soon as I stopped cutting, I allowed my eating disorder to take over again. I basically stopped eating, and when I did eat something, I threw it right back up. This continued for 11 more months; Anorexia became my new vice.

Being thin was a goal I always believed I had to achieve. I felt like the only thing I had to offer any romantic partner was my body, and if I were skinny enough, they would overlook all my fucked-up flaws. Insecurities ran rampant, and the fear of not being perfect haunted me. I was so terrified of sex that in June 2018, I decided to get drunk and get it over with. I had no space for intimacy or vulnerability, and in my mind, if I never had to see them again, they never existed. This was the beginning of some not so great decision-making.

In October of 2018, I entered residential treatment for anorexia. I was there until February 2019. This was when I started writing. I spent months, twenty-four hours a day, seven days a week, working through my sexual trauma, sexuality, emotional history and trauma, and behaviours. It was there that I learned that my worth isn't my weight. I learned that for my brain to function, I need to eat, and that society's diet culture is fucked up and WRONG!! I learned that I am not any of my illnesses. I fell in love with someone for the second time. I felt absolutely no shame here; it was a place where I felt utterly understood. It also felt like, the hardest thing I ever experienced.

After I finished the program, I went to live with my aunt. Being at home was too much of a leap with no one there holding me accountable but myself. It was the start of a long and uncomfortable, but good road. The open, nonjudgmental support I received allowed me to practice being authentic, and that was crucial. I Learned that not everyone agrees with my opinion, but that does not make mine wrong and that fighting with those I love isn't always bad. I also realized that I can only choose to change for myself and not others. Another significant awareness is that communication keeps me sane. I was given the freedom to be authentically me, and that led me to safely explore sex, relationships, connection, and on some level, the loneliness I sometimes feel. Mistakes and accidents happened, but I experienced a lot of growth.

Finally the day came when I felt ready to move home. It happened fast, and I wanted to start pursuing my career and educational goals. I was hired for full-time work in Vancouver and loved it. The job entailed some weird scheduling and long hours, and over time I started letting my mental health slip a little bit. But, it was just that at first – a little bit. Along with the stress of work and some dating choices, my anxiety peaked, which led to the start of a ride downhill. To this day, I still find myself starting to slip. Eventually, I came out of it a few months later, after some ass-kicking from my loved ones. I continue to have good and bad days. The difference now is that I want to have a future; I know it will not be perfect, but that is okay. Imperfection is what I want.

IN REPAIR

FROM EXISTING TO LIVING

VOLUME I

I started writing as a way to express my inexpressible feelings.

Volume I encompasses my journey from
September 2018 – March 2019.

At this point, I just entered a residential treatment program.
I used all my free time to write and discovered I loved it.

~

The waves of pain come crashing in
With them they take away my light
I can no longer see a future
Where the waves don't drown me
So I let myself get swept away
Hoping that the depths of the abyssal ocean
Will match the colour of my craving soul

~

I feel like drowning in my own pain
Just letting go.
I want to sink into the comfort of oblivion
Suffering is too much
And satisfaction doesn't come often enough
My pain is pure
Even the sun cannot paint me golden
A sea of overwhelming misunderstanding

~

You throw your coins into a wishing well
Wishing for something happy
I throw my coins into a wishing well
Hoping for something a little more dark
For something to match the smoldering pain
That torched who I was
I used to wish for happy things like you
Now that's not true
All I can do is dream about those days
But they're getting harder to remember
Every day the light lessens
Until no more can get through
I hope that day comes soon
For the day I can be free
Of all this reminiscing

~

I long for the freedom
to think for myself
but I'm stuck in the ease of sickness
choosing to hold onto the pain
aware of each time I empty my stomach
aware of each time I deprive my body of nourishment
and my bones of growth
feeling hungry is familiar
self-loathing is perpetual
but hunger pains eb and flow
so what's a little more hunger going to do

~

I can feel myself feeling something
But I can't remember
How to feel
The pain of emotion drowns out my thoughts
My mind obstructs my feelings
To protect me from the ultimate damage
Of falling devastatingly in love
So just don't tell me you're in love
Because you'll be left lonely
I can't handle the truth
Those words won't survive
They'll get twisted up inside my tragic mind
My heart feels like an abandoned building
Caught in a storm of acid rain
It strips me of my exoskeleton
And leaves me bare and wilting
The judgment has left me forgotten and vacant
Deserted in the cold
Vulnerability leaves my soul naked
And I cannot survive in the cold

~

You call me sweet thing
But the only thing sweet about me is my orgasms
And I give those to myself
Because you're too busy worrying
About whether I meet your standards of beauty
My body is not a toy for you to enjoy
Simply because I'm a woman.

~

I want to let my feelings out
But I'm in a public place
Surrounded by people
Drowning out my space

~

I think she suffers for the thrill of it all
It's the only thing that can't disappoint her
Everything else has the possibility to ruin her
Just a little bit more than it did before
She knows that it hurts
She feels like it's all she's worth
Exactly what she deserves
Suffering is her security blanket
Its tattered and broken
It still serves the same purpose
To keep her tethered to the ground

~

I dig a grave for my secrets
Hoping they won't be found under these mound of dirt
But all my secrets won't fit in a single grave
I need a whole graveyard
So I might as well bury my body
Maybe one day I'll turn to treasure

~

I feel so alone
In my fight for liberation
When only part of me believes I can live
Without this dictation
Of my brain's introspection
So I sit in isolation and frustration
As all the voices in my head
Tell me I'm better off dead

~

How can I look in the mirror and love myself?
If I can't see my hip bones?
That would mean I'll be forever alone
How can I eat if I don't deserve it?
A flat stomach and a thigh gap are easier to love
How can I accept my story
If it's written in red all over my body?
How can I get better when all I want
Is the pain that stops everything?
The safe familiar freefalling of pain and punishment
Self-hated is my version of self-love
It protects me from obliterations
No one can hurt me If I hurt myself worse
Living for someone else isn't living
But it's the only thing that keeps me off the ledge
That leads me to the freefalling freedom of nothing
Because nothing is better than anything
I protect myself with a razor blade
Making sure I can never let anyone in
Scarring my skin into art with the intent of isolation
Letting me continue the cycle of self-hate and self-
affirmation of how worthless I am
How can I tell them they destroyed me?
How they took a perfect house and smashed it
Into broken little pieces
I can't put myself back together if each time I try
I get cut by a shard reminding me that I'm nothing
I don't fit into a tiny shiny perfectly ideal box with a bow

~

I write out my thoughts on blank pages
Letting the ink bleed through
Pretending the page is my skin
And the ink is the blade

~

The world spins until every last ounce of oxygen escapes her body
Floating up through the atmosphere
With it taking the connection she craves
What she used to be is now gone

~

I physically empty my body
And accidentally empty my feelings
Spilling into the bathroom sink
Along with a piece of my self-worth
And whatever was left from the last time I ate
Yesterday

~

The agony persists even in my dreams
Imprisoned in my own wreckage of my mind
Twisting and contorting trying to escape
As loneliness flows through my veins painting my body
Leaving me to float through each day

~

I can feel tears rolling down my face
But I'm numb inside
All you wanted was for me to love you
But I couldn't
The façade of anger and suffering
Masked the painful chasms of self-loathing
Among each part of my body and soul

I was drowning in my own pain
With each odious occurrence of an invalidating encounter
The water got pushed further down my throat
Filling up my whole existence with emotional turmoil

I couldn't keep my eyes open
I wanted to sink into the deep comfort of oblivion
Stuck in a sea of overwhelming understanding
Suffering was too much
And satisfaction didn't come often enough
So I was blind to your own suffering

~

I sit with wanting to die
Wanting to erase myself from existence
I can't take away the mess I made
So I numb myself to float away
Harming myself until I feel dead inside
So my outside matches my inside
Then maybe someone will notice the unconceivable
Pain that consumes me
I hold my heart in my hand while its barely beating
This world sucks the life out of my already fragile self
My lungs breathe in clean air
Turning to poison
I slowly smother myself with each breath
Proving almost fatal

~

I see something different in you
A spark in your eye that swirls deep through your soul
One that others don't have
One that tells the word you're a fighter
A freedom breaker
For the ones who still have chains tied to their ankles
Instead of bells

~

Feelings of pain last for eternity
Hunger pains eb and flow
I'm entertained by my own sadness
Riding the high of my lonely starving body
A body that will only keep me afloat for one more day
If I keep treating it this way

~

Looking back through old memories
Leaves a sad smile on my face
Along with the bitter taste of sadness
I know you love me but you're too scared to feel alive
And you would
With me by your side

~

Control comes with shoving my finger down my throat
Addiction comes with having to

~

When she falls
She falls in the dark
So no one can see her bleed
A flick of the light switch controls her pain
And when the light comes back on
Her screams turn back into smiles
But over time the light burns for too long
And the heat turns her wiring brittle
Starting a fire in her soul

~

I turn off the light in the bathroom
So I can sit in a dark room
And pretend I am fine
Continuing to empty my feelings out through my throat
Trying to convince myself a lower number will make me feel
alive

~

Neither of us wants to blame the other
So both of us blame ourselves
It's easier to hate myself
So the pain of realizing you aren't enough
Doesn't shatter my heart beyond repair
But now I'm realizing it might have been you
And it's starting to hurt too much
I sit with nothing
As it slowly breaks me inside and out
I can't understand why you couldn't just love me
But maybe you did
And maybe you just loved me a little too much

~

Unwanted images flood my mind
As I look at my porcelain skin
My fingers glide over the warm flesh
Aching to leave another scar
Aching to fill my hearts vacancy
Looking for unattainable validation

~

My sexual orientation isn't a show
So no.
This isn't for your pleasure
It's for mine.
I can kiss her
And love her
And fuck her
just for myself
So I run my finger across her red painted lips
Leaving them parted
Just so ours can softly connect
leaving the lingering taste of something unfamiliar behind
touching her body with the delicate caress of a feather
I'll listen to her draw in each breath
Tangled in the soft satin sheets
Sinking into the mattress
Sweat dotting her skin
And no,
I will not once think of you.
But I'll be thinking of her when I touch myself

~

I long to feel alive
But I don't think I can survive
To be strong means to fight
But I have no energy for this lifelong battle

~

I saw everything in you
And you saw the world in me
Until you rubbed your eyes
The blur fading into sharp colour

~

My heart isn't broken
Just torn
And a little bit worn
By the hands of others
But most of all
From the love I couldn't give myself

~

You hold onto who you thought I'd become
But the sharp inhale of air you suck into your lungs
When I walk by
Shows that I'm strong
That you were wrong

~

Being emotional shows power
So don't call me a delicate fucking flower
I reappear each year

~

My destiny is middle ground
Not at the bottom of the ocean
Or flying too close to the sun
It's to pick up my feet
And land firmly on the earth
The elements test my patience
If my armour is ready for the fight
I need to let go of my beliefs
The tether doesn't have to be so tight

~

I'm stuck in the realm of your rule
Trapped in the walls of your kingdom
You're still lingering in the corners of my mind
Subtly speaking words of wisdom
As if you own me
Not enough to overwhelm me
But just enough that I still notice your presence
Just enough to remind me of the fact
That I'm not yet truly free

~

You loved me in all the ways I couldn't love myself
But it wasn't enough
And it won't be
Until I love the parts of me
Even you didn't want to see

~

A sudden downpour of thoughts fill my mind
Thoughts of weakness and self-blame intertwined
Uninvited and not asked for
I can't hit rewind on my life
But I can learn to redesign

~

Truth shattered the glass ceiling of my shame
It broke my boundaries on blame
And held my feet to the fire that burned within
Stripping me bare of all the secrets that I thought guarded my soul
Leaving only what is real in the reflection of my mirror
One that I'm not familiar with
One full of suffering, pain and loneliness
A girl in fragmented pieces
Only truth will put her back together
Only truth will let me learn to love her

~

I hide under societies rules for women
I look for belonging in the gap between my thighs
In the loose fit of my jeans
Between each empty space in my ribcage
Under each layer of makeup
In each strand of straight hair
With each fake smile

~

Short skirts aren't an invitation
For me to open my legs
I'm not a doe
It's not open season

~

Fairy tales are a false reality
But that doesn't mean I can't be happy
Body positivity and self- love are what will save me
Not a knight in shining armour

~

I feel at home now
In the same body
With the same brain
Even though there is no physical change
I am not the same
I finally let myself be
So now I can be free

~

White lines cover parts of my smooth skin
A tattoo of growth
Inside and out
Blooming into a woman

~

Oh baby I see your mask
But promise me you'll try
To untangle those thoughts
That keep you a prisoner of your own mind
You haven't lost yourself
Just searching for the pieces that have floated away
But don't go searching in the wrong place
I hope you look within
Because you'll rise again one day
Don't ask me why
All you need to know is that your wings help you fly

~

In the midst of suffering
I let the light hit my face
And tell myself
Everything is going to be okay

~

Sarah Lynn

VOLUME II

When I finished treatment and went to live with my aunt,
I started forming a life worth living.

What that included was working, getting a kitten,
therapy, and writing.

Volume II of my journey took place from
March 2019 to October 2019.

~

From the grave of my shattered bones flowers grow
The soil rich with the compost of my pain
Under the warmth of the atmosphere
My new body takes shape
Soft and flawed sculpted from truth and beauty
Inside and out it's a fresh start

~

Beautiful lightless depression casting a shadow onto my bed
I don't want to be a fool anymore
It's time to let go of sorry
It's time to tell a different story
There is nothing I believe more
That peace of mind is in a piece of my mind
Healing doesn't exist in the behind
I drink from the well of bad decisions
Knowing exactly what it will do
I crave dysfunction the same way I crave a hug
It provides me with the same feeling
Flowers on vines
Electric power lines leading my way
I stumble upon broken art
Reminding me of my broken heart
Washing away in the river
No clear path to heaven
In overgrown weeds of beauty
Heaven is for the untouched souls of sickness
Wait,
That doesn't exist

~

Maybe home can be my body again
A new coat of paint on the walls will only cover my scars
Not to fix and mend them
But I'm dusting away the dirt
And the shine is starting to show
For now it's a place
But soon, it will be home

~

I'm angry for all the women
Who grew up not trusting it's okay to have faults
Believing they must be flawless
I'm angry for all the men
That are being taught to be a man is to be without emotion
Only strong and approachable
Who decided that everyone must be the same?
It has created a world full of mundane
I'm angry for all the women
Who live in fear of being treated unfairly
We are not comparable to anything involving mediocrity
Nor should anyone else be
I'm angry for all the men
That had their nurturing nature suppressed
Because others couldn't handle the judging
Why are these standards created
When they aren't reachable
Without giving up a vital piece of themselves
I'm angry for you
And all you have to go through

~

Feminism isn't taboo
Mainstream culture isn't always true
You don't need a crown
Or a princess gown
To be beautiful
You can have pale lips
Stretch marks on your hips
With freckles dotting your skin
Pretty isn't who you are
Don't believe words coming from someone
Who hides their own scars
Don't believe words coming from a culture
That suppresses any form of originality

~

Why are my body parts compared to fruit?
I'm only ripe through a certain season
I have an expiry date
Only acceptable when in a presentable state
Speak the truth and say it loud
My blouse can be untucked
My skirt hiked up
It's still not an invitation or a reason
I'm not telling you I'm ripe and in season
Speak the truth and say it loud
Refusing your advances doesn't make you less of a man
It means I don't want to continue to be chased
Boys will be boys is a phrase
And excuse
Rotten deep to the core
Speak the truth and say it loud

~

I wanted so badly to belong to something
Or someone
But belonging led me to bad decisions
Until all I wanted
Was to belong to myself

~

Sitting on the floor of my closet
Making art
But I can't come out
Until the writings done
Because silence breaks already broken hearts
And I can't be who I really am
Until I come out

~

Compensation
is not the key
To fulfillment

~

We all have places of aching
Some more easily hidden than others
Take a breath
Breathe in the beautiful divine
While great pain tries to hide under the roses
Disguising itself as something that needs to be held onto
Thorns can exist
Yet roses don't need their thorns to stay in bloom

~

The voice in my head
Doesn't pay rent
So why can't I seem to evict it?

~

I'm caught in a weak spot
My thoughts know how to contradict one another
Distorting the truth
Blurring the lines
Leaving me insecure and unsure
I'm not sick anymore
Only a few symptoms present themselves
When opportunity is shown
Sometimes it's often
Sometimes it's not
It depends on what state of being
I find myself in
Always looking for reasons
For reasons why you love me
Or why you don't
Never landing on enough of either

~

Getting older means outgrowing my fears
Only to grow into bigger ones
I'm still scared of the dark
But it's a different kind of darkness
One that looms when the sun rises
And dissipates when the sun sets
A dimply lit world
From the light of the moon that lets me hide
The only place I can find peace
With a sliver of peace of mind

~

I feel a little lonely sometimes
Not alone
But lonely
Unusually broken inside
This happens once in a while
For a reason that doesn't come to mind

~

4:00 am and the lights are still on
Basking in the warm comforting glow of gloominess
At the core of my fear lays love
You might leave me or you wont
Lingering in the I don't knows
Maybe one day I won't be chosen
I don't want to change you
But will you grow without me?

~

Long are the nights I lay awake
Where anxiety takes up residence in my body
Spinning circular heads through my head
Letting me spin out of control

~

Insecure isn't a feeling anymore
It's a character trait
Vanity won't change that
Acceptance might
But in this moment nothing feels right

~

My tears refuse to fall
Just like you refuse to love me
Now I'm all messed up
Thinking about what's wrong with me
When the truth is you are the inadequate one

~

I hope my thoughts of you aren't true
Thinking about you leaves me ice cold and blue
Tears of dismay slip from the corner of each eye
Big enough to form a pool at my feet
Drowning me in a river of fear
Fogging up my thoughts until I'm consumed
Now were just a mirage of ghost stories
You're the ghost and I'm the story

~

What is the point my body weight is making?
Why am I making this happen again?
Oh that's right,
You aren't worth eating for
No
Being fat won't get you love other than from the
Bottom of the ice cream bowl
No
Ugly isn't something you can fix but the weight
On your stomach is
No
A gap between your thighs looks better than
The kindness in your eyes
No
You wouldn't be single if you weren't so annoying
No
All the lingering gazes are good enough praise so
Don't fucking eat
No
Sex and lonely nights feel better when you're thin so don't give in
No
Life will be fixed if you hit size extra thin
I starve myself to feel in control
In control of what?
Control obviously doesn't exist
When I'm unable to feed my starving body
What is weight?
Just a number that's made up by the gravitational
Pull to the earth
In that case wouldn't it be better to take up more space?

I want to get better
Reminding myself life can be good
Happy can come from fueling with food
So why does the scale matter?
Uh oh the scale isn't accurate, why?
Because it's not a number I like
Shame surrounds the number if it climbs higher
Because why?
That means I'm fat? Out of control? Yes.
So I search for ways to control my biological needs to eat
Half restriction is harder
As I start to give my body permission to eat a little bit
The biological need takes over and I can't stop eating
Especially when I'm alone
I'm scared
But you are okay
It's okay
Yes
Your weight isn't your worth
Yes
The love you show your soul will be seen and returned even if by
your own self at first
Yes
Beautiful isn't defined by magazine cover pages
Yes
And kind eyes are more beautiful than bony thighs
Yes
Being single has nothing to do with your appearance
Yes
People stare because they're scared not impressed

Yes
Sex can feel like something special
Yes
Extra thin isn't a thing
Eat because you can't live without it
I long for my stomach to be empty
I long for my BMI to be a little bit less
If my body I empty
I won't feel empty
So I play around with the number on the scale
It's a game of how low can I go
The number on the scale determines if I can get laid
If I'll be loved
Id turn myself inside out
If it meant I could be weigh a milligram less
Only the weight of a feather will do
That will get me the attention I crave
When the compliments pile up.
I can cash them in
Maybe I'll treat myself to a few extra calories
But wait,
I can't turn those compliments untrue
So I eat until I'm blue in the face
And then I empty it all out
Letting the emptiness of my stomach fill up with
Shame for what I've just done
The hate crime I have just committed on my body
Treating my body like a temple has turned into
Treating myself like trash

~

I'm too fat
So I turn to the next fad
Convinced that will give me the capacity
To live within the walls of my body

~

Wow a whole drink for 10 calories
I think yes
Maybe that's what I'll consume for the next few days
To lose a few pounds
To lose my place
I've spent this whole life running
Nothing in front of me is ever close enough
Turning into an illusion as soon as my fingers brush
As real as a model with an airbrushed face
Now that everything feels wrong
I want this empty space
Permanently situated behind my rib cage

~

Calorie counting kept her sane
Being sick freed her from the burden of pain
It let her maintain adolescence a little longer than most
When the real world scared her
So she thrived on the seemingly innocent compliments
The naivety of normal people as they say
"you haven't eaten today I wish I could be that good"
What they don't know is
She replayed images of herself eating all day
All the while sipping diet soda
Pretending her body didn't need energy to survive
A fake smile for show
The bubbly girl never faltered
She always strived for perfection
Never wanting any bad attention
Never wanting trouble
Like she did in her lunch box and princess days
She was always told she was pretty and beautiful
Why not intelligent and curious and colourful
Maybe then her pride would come from her accomplishments
In the educational department
Not the lingerie department

Isn't it ironic,
that thinner rhymes with dinner?

~

I sleep in different beds
In the name of exploration
Letting someone take up my space
Thinking it will fix this empty feeling
They move on
Each time a part of me doesn't
Connection is nothing how I imagined
We didn't take it slow
I didn't want to
Until suddenly I took a step back
Leaving when I didn't want to

~

My depression has some confessions
Apparently it has a mind of its own
I'm not actually sad I'm choosing to feel this way
I don't feel anything because I am numb
But that's just because it's fun not to feel
Overthinking takes up too much time
I overthink into a spiral
One that can't ever come to fruition
Yet it manages to occupy my entire existence
At least that's what my depression tells me
Being too much to handle has always been obvious
And I was too oblivious to notice
So I return to my bed
Where I can be alone in my loneliness
It's not like I'm loved in any way
At least that's what my depression tells me
I beg at its feet to let me feel the way I used to
The response is an amused laugh
"honey that was never you"
With that I go back to my blanket of shame
Intertwined into each fiber are my insecurities
Weighing me down

~

My heart beat lowering with every echo off my chest
While I lay in the bathtub pretending I am dead
Letting the water surround my skin
Spilling over the sides of this porcelain human vase
Spilling over my porcelain skin
Why am I still cold
In a pool of warmth
Arguing with both sides of my mind
To sink or swim
In a body of water barely deep enough to drown in

~

When did I become a vessel of pleasure
Supplying my body for the happiness of another
To use and abuse in the name of sensual connection
The only thing connected about us is your body in mine
Do you even care if I'm having fun
You saw it on a screen
The girl was screaming
When he was ignoring her self-esteem
So obviously id like it
That's why you didn't ask
Carelessness isn't consent
Its reckless
Assumptions get you in trouble
Stop and think what this purpose is serving
The only one I see is the patriarchy

~

My tears go anywhere the wind blows
Letting nature be my medicine
Breathing in a breath of fresh air
Letting my dreams run wild
As I lay in the desolation of this worlds landscape
Just asking for a sign
That human tenderness still exists

~

Why am I addicted to bad habits
they seem to find me
Or maybe I'm looking for them
Trying to find an excuse
To get some kind of attention
That will fulfill my need to be adequate

~

I will fight this
I will beat this
I will be brave
I will become me again

~

I want to cry
I mean full body cry
The type where salty tears blind me
The type where I can't breathe or think
The type that lets emotional pain tighten every
Muscle in my body
I need to give myself permission to break
That's the only way ill learn I am strong enough to be okay

~

Sleeping alone lets my dreams run wild
When all I want is a warm body next to mine
I'll settle for someone who isn't you
If it calms the storm inside
Even if I can't remember their name
From a few hours before

~

Self-worth fills the void your body used to
So I touch myself to the thought of anything but you
I touch myself to the thought of being cared for
Sparred the pressure you inflicted in the wrong places
Not spared of my own self-inflicted pressure
That I know brings me pleasure
Slow and steady because I want to get off
Not fast and hard
To please your porn fantasy
To get you hard again
For the fourth time
As I'm still here
Again and again
Not because I expect to enjoy it
But because I expected for sex to be like this
Not for me

~

We had nothing and everything all at once
Time is fading
Taking away what we know
Changing our path through every moment of the day
There is no need to fight it
Everything is alright
Change lights the way to new life

~

Lonely and broken is how I've experienced life
Conditioning tells me I can't ask for help
Burdening is unacceptable
Weep silent tears instead
So saying this doesn't feel comfortable
I love you and I feel betrayed
Betrayed sometimes by your lack of patience
Instead of "you know what to do"
Turn it into "how can I help"
Instead of "we can't keep doing this"
Turn it into "why do you think this keeps happening"
I feel scared
Why can't I cry
Is this what's keeping me up at night?
Why am I letting you down?
What am I looking for?
Something you can't give

Something only I can give to myself
A heart completely whole
I miss feeling close to you
Not in space
But in connection
How is it possible you love someone so messed up
I didn't feel mothered I didn't feel loved
Internally I wasn't enough
I think I've finally figured out what I need
Sometimes advice is lost on an anxious brain
Could you just say
Babe it's okay
You have no obligation or commitment to love me
I think it's time to admit I didn't think my life through
Imagining it'd end early on
Now I don't know what to do

~

Thoughts vibrate at a different frequency in my mind
Serotonin levels as if on cocaine forever
Just get out of bed they say
You tell me I'm fine
I tell me I'm fine
That the only prescription I need is prescription sunshine
I'd rather fill my body with love
Not men
My blood is colourless from sadness
If it's not sex its drugs
If it's not alcohol its starvation
Nutrient deprivation in all the forms
Gives me a reason to rely on anyone but myself
Tears fall from the sky
But it's not god who is crying
It's the angels of past loved ones
Weeping at how I am treating myself
Like a weather drought
Greenery and shrubs captured by mud
Still blooming their best
Different love of different fun
Lasting not long enough
I live my life in muted ways
Scared of blinding myself

~

A little girl full of perfection
A little girl full of blown up expectations
Can't create anything but hard learned lessons
A version of myself made up of by everyone else
Finally I felt like me today
I feel like me
I feel like figuring her out
For the first time in years
However different from what I expected her to be
I resonate with what I see in the mirror
Looking in the mirror I saw who I was becoming
The version of me
I never thought I would be
I didn't recognize her exactly
But I liked her
I was curious
The soft curves
The soft skin
The energy within
Especially the painted lines
Reminding her to be
Whoever she needs
It's okay to choose who she wants to be
Falling in love with whatever that might be

~

Pleasure for one isn't as fun
It'd be better if your hands were all over me
So I touch myself to the thought of you
Even though I have a million other things to do
Sitting alone gives me plenty of time
For images of you to float through my mind
Pages and pages of unwritten text
Just waiting to be read

~

Touch Is what I crave
Close nights and open mindedness
Sharing our deepest fears out in the clear
Sinking into the sweet smell of your skin
Lingering a little close than friends would
In my dreams I imagine your breath cooling my skin
Are we there yet?
The part where lust becomes love?
Will we ever be?
You didn't need to tell me I was the best you ever had
I felt it

~

I let you into my body
Under the pretense of pleasure
Under pretenses of your respect for others
A little fun never hurt anyone too badly
Right?
The space you took up was just that
Fun.
Nothing more nothing less
I thought you knew I deserved some say
Or were your needs more important?
Connection took a back seat to your erection
Leaving you to reject permission
Leaving me to question whether I'm just
An object of affection
Defective in the department of being a woman
Having bad sex is now a rite of passage
Blowjobs are a badge of honor
But not for me because I am a woman
It's just an expectant thing for me to do
I'm a prude if I don't
And dirty if I do
I'm real lucky if you return the favor
But I don't hold my breath because it's much too taboo

~

A punishment comparable
to a kid getting his hand caught in the cookie jar
what is that you might ask?
Months and weeks in a cell for violation that lasts a lifetime
It's a life sentence for me
It's an inconvenient moment in time for you
Consequently paving the way
For a belief that the way I chose to dress my body
Is enough to excuse your poor choices
My tight dress is a ticket of admission
To this one woman show
And the show isn't even private
When I don't have a say in who pays
It's just a game
One that I wasn't invited to play
One I'm required to show up to anyway

~

I don't hate love
I just rather make love
Than be in love
My body still craves touch
My mind still wants lust
I can't handle any more misplaced trust
Your desire is designed for me
As your fingers remove each piece of lace
Feel my skin and kiss my thigh
Give me the feeling of being high
Drag your finger across my hip
Dipping a little lower
The color of my complexion gives everything away
My body warm
Heating the sheets
Burning down the world around us

~

Situations get misread
My emotions leave me upset
Words get over said
Vulnerable to opinions
It's so easy to get misled
In this mind full of anxieties
Too many uncertainties
Too many insecurities
I'm no good with words
Speaking comes easy
In the form of touch

~

I set fire to my soul
Burning away all traces of me
Leaving the framework of who I used to be
Rebuilding will start slowly
This time I refuse to use old pieces
New beginnings need new knowledge
I finally discovered there is no change overnight
It takes time and perseverance to be alright

~

Today was normal
Sadness didn't hang around
Anxiety didn't show up to the party uninvited
Loneliness was stopped at the door
Not allowed to crash this party
No one left to blame anymore
Trust is earned
Time and time again
These party crashers have been discounted
Just because they show up
Doesn't mean they are to be trusted

~

Feeling is something I have not yet found peace with
So hold onto me as I let it flow freely
Freely through my body
Trying to figure out the feelings
The unrecognizable states of mind
Guiding my way
My mistake
It was never me who chose to be this way

~

I was drunk
He was
Fun
It didn't matter that I didn't know him
It mattered that I wanted to be touched
No breakthroughs now
Just spinning around and around
Why is this the one thing I can't change
I'm not afraid of the world
I'm just afraid to grow up
That's why I like older dates
They're grown ups
So I don't have to be
I was high
I knew it wasn't a lie
When he told me he was forty
And what's wrong with that
If it was my choice too
It happened with a preconceived record
Or stories saved up in my head
To look back at it and kind of regret
It's always a good idea at the time
Until I wake up the next morning
And remember who I was trying to be
The night before
I wanted to be the girl with no trauma
No backlash on her habits or old drama
Normal and pretty
Because I grew up thinking pretty and sexy were the same thing

~

Trying to forget the flaws and traumatic applause
That has shown up in places of my body
Now I see how they got in
Those places of aching

~

Sadness weighs down in my veins
Pulling everything away
Everything I used to do for validation
Came from complex unsure behaviour
Whatever flavor of the day I was feeling
Thinking the only way to be seen
Was to feel it all on the outside
Be it all on the inside

~

Sometimes I miss the days
Where my diet consisted of chain smoking and coffee
Where my days were spent in bed
Sleeping life away
Thoughts stuck in my head
Too sick to exist
To well to be dead
Not capable of conservational niceties
Exempt from human activities
Void of ability
Never a new city
Never a new place
Could change that
Immune to conflict
Immune to feelings
amuse to life
Nothing left to sacrifice
More use to science than this human filled world

~

In favor of fitting in
An apple a day keeps the doctor away
So eating only two a day will be okay
Don't eat anything else
And you'll lose a few pounds
She kept that up
Led her to believe she could achieve her dreams
If there was a little bit less of her
A smaller body equated to bigger dreams
Nothing could get in her way
Except maybe starve brain syndrome
But that's just a small price to pay
For perfection

~

Our eyes are imbedded with an infinite number of images
How we should be
Who we should be
Where does the process of learning who we are start
Nothing ever stays the same
In the process of figuring that out
When the stories we are told
Nothing is good enough but gold

~

Isn't it ironic?
I'd give my soul
To feel anything at all

~

Mourning something that still has the capacity to exist
Seems like an impossible achievement
All day I work on a life of fulfillment
Turning within when I have ignored all my basic needs
Yet stuck making me more of a failure

~

I crave something sharp
To carve out a familiar reality
Take me to a place I remember so vividly
One soft stroke at a time
Opening a space for my emotions to escape
On sliver at a time

~

My eyes are tired
Of hearing what my brain says
And seeing something completely different

~

Survival mode is a setting for people locked in dysfunction
And I embody dysfunction
Or should I say I used to
Now I just embody different men
Being a slut makes more sense than my
abandonment issues do
Amplifying that all problems can be fixed by men
Each dimple and wrinkle and freckle placed
Perfectly to his taste
I like black lace
And I like a man's ass
But I don't go around grabbing it
In what world did my looks give permission to
touch my body
Consent is only a yes
What if I was considered "ugly", would I be grabbed then?
We all know the answer to that question is yes
I go out anyway, drinking to be okay with being touched
By okay I don't mean that it's not wrong
I say okay just to tolerate it
Or should I say my ego tolerates it
I know I shouldn't
I know I'm worth more than some scoreboard of hot or nots
And whether I'm hot or not isn't determined by a
man's afterthought
I'm not a side piece
That's the job of my one night stand
I'm talking about the drawer beside my bed
Not a date I take home for the night

~

I'm not a little girl anymore
Lust is knocking at my door
Like it never has before
Everything about this brings me freedom
Knowing I can do something right
The freedom of growing up
Finally realizing my own skin
Should be touched like air
My own bones don't need to be broken
For the fun of someone else
Saying no is okay
Attention isn't everything
I can be my own pleasure
Better than a lover
Knowing what I like first
comes first
Darling nothing is a waste
Except for sexual distaste
In the form of being unsafe

~

When I feel like this
It's from my own fingertips
High from bringing myself to the edge
The borderline of my skin within
I rather drink cheap wine alone
Than be sober and not have anyone to touch me
At least when I'm drunk I have time to care about my body
The feel between my own sheets
Feels better than you ever did

~

To my past lovers who couldn't be true
Who tried to be true
To my past lovers who used their touch selfishly
Not for me
To my past lovers who lacked boundaries
Thinking I belonged to them
Thinking of me as only a body to use
To my past lovers you were never special
I hope you digress from a path of inattentiveness
I forgive you
But someone else won't

~

I put my hands on myself
Thinking of you
Wishing it could be true
Crying to that touch
Even when its bringing me pleasure
Even if it's for the better
What happens if this is all I settle for
Just the touch of my own hand to skin
Not letting anyone in
Because submission is easier than admitting
to wanting intimacy
Dominance is to let go of permission
When I can't acknowledge my own ignition points
When I can't honour them
Even though I knew you would
Now I'm ready for you to feel me
Be with me
But timing doesn't work out
I have nothing to let out
Sleeping with others
To fill where you are not
Maybe that's why I let others touch me in public
Fuck me in public
Because it's a show of being wanted
Something you didn't end up wanting
Showing myself I'm worth wanting
Now it's turned into something haunting
Leaving me alone and thinking

~

Believe me when I say
I want you in every way
I want you to stay.
Can you tell me,
what are we doing here?
You don't find me weak
You don't manipulate me
I'm not used to that
Vulnerability doesn't make you run the other way
So I keep searching for reasons to let you go
To let myself off the hook from heartache
Clearly the reasons aren't reason enough
Because you're still here
But so is my fear

~

I look for the red flags
To find an exit bag
A sort of suffocation in a way
My cards were dealt long ago
Everything had been cashed in
It's time to cash out
There is something too flashy about happiness
That seems suspiciously fake
Sending nervous systems into over drive
Nervous of mistakes
Requiring rewiring
To meet new level of the bare minimum

~

Sadness continues to stay present in my body
Through moments of happiness
Maybe it's because suffering is comforting
When it's all I've ever known
To feel nothing seems sweet
Even when nothing comes without a price

~

In my dreams I am free
Pink angel skies remind me I am alive
And the sun soaks up my pain
A dark cloud doesn't follow me around
Raining on my parade
I don't float in fear
Not fearing this thing we call life
Imagination seemed to awake a passion
Slowly seeping into my state of conscience
Turning my dreams into daydreams
Bringing them closer
Waking up stopped hurting
Once I realized
Living is the real heaven

~

You used to love so deeply it took over
Now there is no release for your emotions
Shallow breaths holding everything in
Suffocating the joy of existing right out
Remember the times when it was okay not
To have all the answers
Figuring everything out isn't what life is all about
Just because someone told you something
Doesn't make it true
It's okay to believe your own truth
It's okay for someone else not to
It's not a sign that something is wrong with you
Good intention don't excuse hurt feelings
You can unwire others voices from inside your own head
By remembering being you is all that was ever meant

~

Blooming like a lily under the moon
Is what your spirit is doing
As I watch you toy with connection
Figuring out what makes it blossom
I just hope you stay kind to your body
Listening to the whispers of your heart
More is always what you deserve
Right now and forever
Take some time to reflect on what you'd like
Remembering only the words of your own soul

~

And suddenly
She was too tired
Too worn out
To let the world slip through her finger tips
In the form of protection
Instead she let society's approval slip through her finger tip
~

I'm proud of myself
Why is that considered vain
I'm not sorry I'm the one who told you no
Now I just feel sorry for you
Throwing yourself a pity party
And whine every time something doesn't go your way
So it's time to let me go
I don't need to carry the weight of your doubt around
Its holding me down

~

Looking through old photos gets me emotional
Seeing as if I were someone else
Gives me a touch of perspective
Shining the light on what to fight for
Sometimes I'll catch a glimpse of my own reflection
Untainted for a second
Skinny doesn't look pretty
Under a microscope

~

I'm sorry for your loss
Loss of self-identity
Loss of who friends were supposed to be
Loss of time for making memories
What I'm not sorry for is your experience
It showed your capability to show up
It uncovered a need for self-preservation
It reminded you weak is something you are not
Connection built through pain
Came with voices speaking of compassion out loud

~

Instead of her heart
She wore the truth on her sleeve
Deterring the fake and futile
Paving the way for a beautiful life
Full of authenticity and peace

~

In moments of stillness
Remember the you underneath the trauma
The child who's creativity was crushed under the
Weight of others opinions
Who would you be if expression of self wasn't
Looked down upon
Would tears flow freely?
Instead of evaporating?
Remember that feeling of laughter vibrating
Through your bones
Because you went afraid of judgment
As a kid you loved spontaneously, unaware of rejection
You weren't yet taught to believe it was shameful
Think about when you weren't afraid to just be
Before camouflage was praised
When did things change?
Remember the you who was taught to hide
Look back with compassion
You didn't know better
Was your innocence stolen or was that just
What you were told
Could they just possibly have used the wrong words
Did stick and stones really break your bones
Or was it the words
Remember when you used to play pretend
It's called daydreaming now

~

Dear little me
You are loved
Even when you don't feel seen
This world works in ways you don't yet know
Dear little me
You aren't too much
Those who make fun of you
Are missing something
Dear little me
Don't give up
Just because you're different
Doesn't mean wrong
It shouldn't degrade your self-worth
Dear little me
Your smile is radiant
But its okay
If it doesn't always stay this way
Life is messy
Dear little me you aren't alone
No matter the sides of people you are shown
Dear little me
You are a woman
You are a warrior

~

Sarah Lynn

VOLUME III

Self-worth starting to work…

It's like we were born and formed and created in a factory
Unable to learn and form and create uniquely
Growing up in this society
Make up and go out
Stay up late and stay out
Just another body looked at
like a rooftop view
in a sea of "me too's"
now stand ups are standard
going to a bar is the grown up version of toys r us
it's called hook-ups r us
nothing but damaged goods as a woman in this culture
nothing other than a king as a man in this culture
my resistance is inconvenient
compared for a mans need to feel adequate

~

Don't make the mistake
And think that we all will survive
Cut to the chase
We will all die if nothing changes
Drink dark matter
Fall from sacred space
Box up society and sell it to the new god
Sell it to her
She will take care of the mess
That guy left behind
She builds a new world with
Kind
Brave
Love
That's all it takes
Why would you spend your whole life wondering
If you could have used your voice
Despite everything
And use it to light up the sky
I wish that could be true
But my dear
That's a job for god herself

~

There are a lot of things I don't understand in this world
Starting with how I ended up being taught
That pretty was my worth
Not ending with men are taught to go after
Us without consequence
A pans punishment for rape is equivalent to a speeding ticket
And it's my fault for saying no that's not what I was taught
And the most fucked up part of it all
Is that the men thought there was nothing wrong

~

Those bodies I upheld to the standard of
My own romanticism
Were just containers to put all of my emotions in
Maybe that why I was always left feeling empty
Getting caught up in lust pretending it was love
What a lonely way to live

~

Forever there will be us
Together we must enjoy our love
Everything can be left unsaid
We see through the lines of our own skin
Underneath and within
Oh baby
Think about where our lives will lead
Wherever you are
You'll always be in my heart
We don't need touch
To feel each other's immense love

~

I wanna fight like a girl
So please,
Call me a pussy
I'll take it as a compliment
Regardless of how you meant it
My heart
My hips
My body
My lips
None of those belong to you

~

You look happier I keep hearing everyone say
And it's true
I've been feeling less blue these days
Although
There will always be some sort of darkness inside
Still sometimes
I get tired of my mind
Having to put out the fires
My thoughts leave behind

~

I feel the need
To be the old me
The human I used to be a little while ago
Creep back into my spine
Growing slowly into a vine with poisonous potential
Using every questionable decision like a
Fall of rain for hydration
Now I find myself up at night feeling the darkness grow
Wondering what my funeral would be like
Wondering how sick I need to be
For others to love me

~

They see the vacancy behind our eyes
Along with all our silent delusions
Filling up free space
No longer quieted by isolation
I feel like I can see daylight
And then it feels like we start a fight
About nothing
I'm beginning to wonder
Where all this stems from
I have everything I have every wanted
Yet I still feel haunted by the same thoughts
Where does all this come from
If my dreams come true
Why am I still feeling this blue
It's not from the place I thought it was
So now it's just another thing to think about

~

Laying in a full bed
Still feeling lonely
Being touched by two
Still feeling cold
A room full of faces
Drowning in empty
Smiling and shining out on the town
A I of beauty and confidence
A smile here and a grin there
Flirting dangerously
Using it to warm my heart
Using false intimacy to remind myself I
Could possibly be loved
Trying to see the world in one night
While trying to disappear into the night
Pieces of me try to fall into place but they don't fit
When those places are strangers

~

I stay up too late
Hoping to find someone to love
After all these things I've done
When all the memories come swimming back in
I'm young
But I wish I was younger
Back to the worries I seem to be free of now
Where this whole world wouldn't come crashing down
Everything would work out
In the simplest of ways

~

There are too many big dreams
Stuck inside my head
Swirling around unattended
One of them is you
One of them is us
Hoping to make it into a wedding dress
I sit here scared
Wondering how I'm not too much
As you tell me you're so in love
Even after seeing me puke in the bathtub
So you say,
Darling I still look at you in the same way
Just look up and promise me
You won't struggle silently
Even when those things hit from every angle
Just talk to me

~

Do you ever feel like life hurts just a little too much
I don't know how to let go of perfectionism
If it's not perfect I'm not worth it
What is it that I really want
What is it that I get out of being sick
My body aches
My healthy
Functioning body aches
The strength in my arms
The weight of my legs
The soft flesh covering every inch of my skin feels weak
I know I have strength
But this sadness takes it away
Always needing validation of my appearance
Young kids leaving leftovers in their lunch boxes at the
Tender age of seven
To look like the magazine covers
What are we teaching kids
That BMI and muscle definition is the key to successful living
What about intelligence, compassion and hard work?
Is that all being thrown out
Think about how we are effected
In a world full of new faces and new places
With the same old boring grudges
It seems harder now more than ever
To let go and grow
Swallowed up by the what ifs the maybes and the could be's
Nothing is ever enough
We want pretty
We are addicted to pretty

Pretty places, pretty people, pretty things
If we lose hope at least we aren't losing pretty
Juggling the weight of the world turned into
Weighing nothing at all
Baggy clothing hiding what I want
Ironic though isn't it?
I want people to notice yet I hide myself
Shame, blame, self-hate no longer hidden behind
A womanly body
It shows in the form of my skeleton
That's what I seem to want
To show society how fucked up this life of
Perfectionism we lead is
Craving living while simultaneously craving
The look of being dead
Craving being stuck in a hospital bed
Craving skin and bone
Only collar bones
One pound turned into two
Two pounds turned into twenty five
Skinny is the goal for most
Almost dead is the goal for us
Anything but this fucking life
Pillow fights and pjs don't fill my dreams
Instead they're filled with the graves of everyone I love
I'd sooner rather be anorexic forever if it means
I love felt less pain
It's so much easier to be the blame than feel the blame
All those sick minds died for what?
We all have hopes and dreams

They did too
They died from being too thin
But that's not the only reason they died
They died searching for a way to be loved
In their own language
The bigger problem is too many kids are self-medicating
With boys and with girls
With dating and with weighing
With using and abusing and self-deprecation
That's why I crave being skin
Being bone
Sickness to avoid the burn of life
Avoid being alone

~

Yes you love me
But you'll grow tired of what I need
Then who will be here to be you for me?

~

I'm traumatized from trauma I imagine
Trauma that actually hasn't happened yet
All my demons
Taking up creative space
I wake up every day
Wondering how they'll treat me today
Leaving me with rueful looks
In a crowded room
Filled with empty promise
I think it's time I retire
The age old thought that all I could ever be
Is desirable
Maybe I'll try
Feeling loved
For a moment

~

Those things you say
Come from your truth
Your trauma
Not mine
Those thoughts you relay
Came from your anxiety
Your judgment
Not mine
What happened to letting me learn
Your mountain of concern put a stop to do that
And the way I want to make love
Might taste bitter to you
But sex doesn't always have to be about love
Let me be and let me hurt like normal people do

~

Distortion like ripples of water
In my own fantasy
Crying tears of color
Turning into shapes and dreams
Everything is all right
Waking up in this oracle place
Breathing in divine psychedelic lucidity
Feeling like its equivalent to sanity
Believing in every change
Trying to medicate dark thoughts away
Fading them into bright lights and dreams
Paving the way
For new shapes
Praying for a new mind
Or
A new time

~

Don't put your hands on my body
Like you think you know it
Until you do
Only then I'll follow you
Footsteps lost and gone
Fading us together
So kiss me soft
Kiss me wherever I want
Undress me with your eyes
Then undress me with your touch
Letting the cold sheets stroke my bare skin
Warm hands adding fuel to my fire
Yet you're still dressed
For my own pleasure
Leave the lights on
I finally don't have to hide
Don't let go
Until I say so

~

I'm a dream to you
You're my heaven
We both said it
Without saying it
I don't want to let you practice
Without distraction
If that distraction isn't my body
Were both scared
Its scaring me
How much or how little do I let in
So the least amount of damage gets done
Logically I want to take it slow
Emotionally I know
I'm already gone

~

Five foot two
Piercing baby blues
Staring at you
There we sat
On Bedford drive
Wishing we were underneath the Hollywood sign
Every thought running through my mind
Wanting to tell you
In the middle of the traffic lights
Falling in love hurts more than lust ever could
And I'm scared
Of this
Of us
Of falling in love
I just hope I can fall
Without making a sound
For months upon months I've woken up in the same place
In the same headspace
And then one day
Out of the blue
Everything that is you
Broke through

~

When you held my body
And asked for context
I said I didn't know what to say next
So it all came out
In one place
In bits and pieces
Messy and scared
Emotional words without emotion
To disconnect myself from our connection
You didn't try to pick up those pieces
Or put me back together
Honest about your own mistakes
Reminding me
I'm not who I once was
I am the me that I am now
That's all that matters
I think you love me
And it's been 8 days
I think I love you
And it's been 8 days
This isn't lust
Maybe not even love
Just a deep understanding

~

We're getting there
My mind can't make up the words
It scares me all too much
The little things
The big things
And everything in between
Because I've never been anyone's girlfriend
Just the girl they've been fucking
Or the girl they might have loved
Not the one they wanted to keep
I like you as a friend
I like you as a lover
I'm hoping forever
Please
As long as we take this minute by minute
Day by day
We should be okay
I think we have something that could bloom

~

Cognitive process seems slower
When I'm sitting with you
Slowly thinking why this works
While you sit there and stare
With everything but pity in your eyes
There is nostalgia I don't feel anymore
Swept up in the building of our love

~

I've never said anyone else's name during sex
But I did then
And it felt comfortable

~

Two glasses in and I feel like arguing
Maybe because we never do
Maybe because I'm insecure
Lost in my own forest of sadness
Losing sleep over miscommunications
Scared this won't work
Scared that it will
So I sabotage us
Or should I say me
At what feels like every opportunity
These days I'm always afraid
Of you
Living for me
Of me
Living for you

~

There we sat
On your kitchen floor
Discussing the scars written on our hearts
And if we'd done it a million times before
And there we sat until the sun set
Beautiful and healing
Leading against the cupboard doors
Wondering if life would ever bring us more

~
v

We don't ever talk small
Our conversations are big
Filled with fire
Filled with love
It's been that way since the beginning
We say what we need to say
Even through a little arguing
We'll always be okay

~

Fairy tales are told to us when we are little
Then we grow up
Throwing it away
Reminding ourselves
To see through the game show
To drop that fake glow
Crashing into our own sort of reality
I want new things with this body
New things I thought I'd never reach
So I didn't bother caring
Now just as soon I have started to
This body is less of art
More a tool to use
Not for men
But for children
And love
For the practice of building my life up

~

Devoted to being skinny is what I used to be
Devoted to empathy
Is what I now strive to reach
There are bigger things in life
That require me to take up much more space
With my body and mind
A new design to find
A new map to make
Letting loose is worth risking a mistake
Taking a breath is worth the give
Keeping to myself isn't worth the take

~

I used to think I paid every week
For you to love me
My secrets are trapped between the walls of your office
All my excuses don't survive in the space between us
And neither does my shame
But now I pay nothing
And you're still here.

~

Sarah Lynn

EPILOGUE

Part of why I got sick and stayed sick, in all the ways I did, was because I felt that I had nothing to lose. Over the years, I adopted the belief that no one could ever fall in love with someone like me. I believed I was too fucked up, too ugly, and too much.

Every dating experience seemed to perpetuate that belief until I met someone in January 2020. I thought this relationship was going to be just another experience. But it was not. I've never loved or been loved by anyone like him. He sees all of me, all of the scars and all the bruises and broken bones.

I will always be up and down. I now know that's how life works, and sometimes that really sucks. I can do things to make my life more steady, like sleeping well, regularly eating, expressing my feelings, taking my meds, setting boundaries, and asking for help when I need it.

To this day, my mental health can distort the way I think. The difference now is that it's easier for me to recognize when that happens. I won't say I am recovered. I don't know if I will ever say that because recovery is a lifelong undertaking. I still struggle and have days and sometimes weeks of relapse. I certainly think about it a lot. When I look back at my past, I occasionally see a warm glow. My mind seems to glamorize it. Sometimes, it pops back up with a harder punch and sometimes, for longer periods than others. There will be times when it is easier to fight back and others when it will be much harder. It' so very frustrating at times, and it is also a constant reminder to properly look after myself.

Being alive seems so powerful to me now. It feels a little sweeter than before. I recognize that I can experience heartbreak, joy, fear, and hope all at the same time. Nothing is permanent; I cannot predict the future, and that is okay. What I failed to realize before was that I have a choice in everything. I can cry, feel deep emotion when a specific song comes on, set boundaries with others, and not feel guilty, and my anger doesn't last for weeks or days anymore. I want to experience all this world has to offer, whether it is extraordinarily wonderful or terrifyingly excruciating.

PRAISE FOR THE AUTHOR

My Dear Sarah

*What a gift it is to know you, to witness your
growth, tenacity, and courage,
and to be touched by the beauty, wisdom, and
strength of your heart.*

*I have watched your make the choice to build a life of
purpose, generosity, and joy,
in spite of the many challenges you faced.*

*You have taught me, and shown in action, that change is possible,
and the transformative power of relationships to heal.*

*Much Love,
From my heart to yours,*

Melissa

ABOUT THE AUTHOR

Sarah Lynn lives in North Vancouver, British Colombia, with her cat, Elliot. She grew up in Deep Cove, the firstborn in a set of triplets. Poetry is one of the passions she enjoys while balancing the chaos and quiet in her mind. Walking, overthinking, playing soccer, crocheting, and eating ice cream right out of the tub, also make that list of passions. Sarah hopes to pursue a career in therapy and continues to write and study.

Dear Lifeteamers

Keep taking care of
all the young souls of the
world.
Enjoy making your own
    Stone Soup in your
    wonderful space ($\frac{t^2}{x}_y$ + ♡)

        Love
            Paul

"Live intensely and
do not accumulate negative
        thoughts" Swami G

STONE SOUP FOR THE SOUL

Other books by Paul Clark:

Stone Soup

for the

Soul

The last self-help book you will ever need

PAUL CLARK

To order additional copies of this book, contact:
Xlibris Corporation
1-888-795-4274
www.Xlibris.com
Orders@Xlibris.com
82900

To all the well-intentioned authors of self-help books
and paraphernalia who pushed me (over the edge)
to write this book:
Dale Carnegie
Stephen Covey
Jack Canfield
Kim Payne
Dr Benjamin Spock

Preface

Over $8.5 billion is spent each year in North America on self-help books. The industry started in 1937 when Dale Carnegie published How to Win Friends and Influence People, followed by Dr. Spock "teaching" mothers how to raise their children. Now we are saturated with these books and yet our divorce rate has skyrocketed, dysfunctional relationships, suicide and loneliness have increased, and a general loss of connection and community is reported. Nobody knows exactly why this has happened but I see a connection between our loss of strong relationships and our need to apply technique to all things. To treat the people in our lives and ourselves like machines that have owners' manuals to guide us like a mechanic to "fix" our problems, is a disaster. It degrades both the giver and the receiver until they are less than human and it doesn't appear to work in the long term.

Love and do as you will
—St. Augustine

One

Relax, trust yourself.
If you need help
reach out to someone
who cares about you.
And
write, draw, paint
or do as you will
to enjoy the next
70 pages . . .

Two

Your turn . . .

Edwards Brothers,Inc!
Thorofare, NJ 08086
18 October, 2010
BA2010292